Saint Vincent de Paul

Servant of charity

BOOKS & MEDIA
BOSTON

English edition copyright © 1999, Daughters of St. Paul

ISBN 0-8198-7023-4

Written by Sister Catherine Ethievant

Illustrated by Augusta Curelli

Translated from the original French by Caroline Morson

Edited and adapted by Mary Cabrini Durkin, OSU
and Patricia Edward Jablonski, FSP

*Layout:*La 7e HEURE

© 1998, Éditions du Signe, 1 rue Alfred Kastler, B.P. 94-67038 Strasbourg

Printed in Spain by Beta-Editorial S/A Barcelona

Other titles in this series:

Saint Anthony of Padua
Proclaimer of the Good News

Saint Colette
In the footsteps of Saint Francis and Saint Clare

Saint Francis of Assisi
God's gentle knight

Saint John Bosco
The friend of children and young people

Saint Thérèse of Lisieux
And the "little way" of love

This is the wonderful story of Saint Vincent de Paul and the great things he did for God and God's people. Before beginning to read it, turn to the back of the book. There you will find an explanation of some words that may be new to you.

Vincent had a big heart. It was filled with many dreams and wishes. At first, Vincent's biggest dream was to become successful and famous. But little by little he opened his heart up to God. And little by little God filled it with a great love called "charity."

This love changed Vincent. It burned inside him like a fire until it just had to spread to others. Vincent began to really *live* these important words of Jesus: "Whatever you do to others you do to me!"

Here is how it all happened....

Long ago, in southern France, not far from the Pyrenees Mountains, the village of Pouy nestled beside the river Adour.

The people there were simple, hard-working farmers, living with the rhythm of the seasons. Some worked in the fields. Others took care of the animals.

On April 24, 1581, the village people smiled when they heard the cries of a newborn baby. The de Paul family was celebrating, for Bertrande and John now had a third child, a little boy called Vincent.
"What a lovely, healthy baby!"
"When will you baptize him?"

The six de Paul children were named John, Bernard, Vincent, Gayon, Mary, and Claudine.
Vincent was the third child. He grew up happily in this family, whose faith was as firm as a strong oak tree.

Soon Vincent could help with the farm work. He learned to plant seeds and cut hay. His Mom, Bertrande, was always teaching her children about Jesus. Vincent learned about God, who created the sky and the earth, and who makes the plants grow with the help of the sun and the rain.

"Mom, look! A little lamb was born this morning."
"He can't stand up on his own yet!"
"Will his mother feed him soon?"
"Yes, Vincent! Thank the Lord, and take good care of the little one."

Long before dawn, Vincent set out with the sheep and pigs. It wasn't easy to find good grazing ground because the land was very swampy. Many times Vincent had to travel a long way. Like the other shepherds, he even had to wear stilts because of all the water and mud!

On the way, while he watched the flock, he loved to catch fish in the river, and listen to the wind in the pine trees and the marshes. He made whistles with reeds that he picked along the way. At noontime, he jumped the hedges with his friends, and played leapfrog or "ambush."

At dinnertime they gathered with the neighbors around a pot of porridge. They all helped themselves. People talked about the terrible wars which were causing so much damage and so many deaths. When would the violence end?

In the evening everyone liked to gather around the fire to tell stories about the life of Jesus. They prayed, "Thank you, Lord, for this wonderful day!"
John and Bertrande noticed how intelligent their third son was and discussed his future.
"Bertrande, Vincent has a sharp mind. How do you feel about sending him to study in town? I really think we should."
"Oh, John, I will miss him so much!"
"So will I. His schooling will also be long and expensive, but we can sell our pair of oxen to raise the money. God will repay us."

The decision was made. Vincent would be sent to continue his education. So at the age of fifteen he left his flocks and the beautiful land of his childhood and moved to the town of Dax to go to school.

He was intelligent and made quick progress. Very soon he managed to find work and pay for his tuition. Even though he was so young, a lawyer hired him to tutor his children.

Vincent had a quick temper. He thought he was important, and he let his success go to his head. One time he was even ashamed of the way his father looked, because Mr. de Paul limped and didn't have fine clothes to wear. This incident was something Vincent was sorry about for the rest of his life.

In 1600, when he was only twenty years old, Vincent was ordained a priest. He was sure he would be a success!

Vincent moved from one place to another looking for an assignment which would make him famous and help him to meet important people.
These were difficult years, filled with adventures! Once he went to Rome on a pilgrimage. Another time his money was stolen, but he chased the thief and managed to have him put in prison.

When he went to Paris, Vincent became the chaplain for Queen Marguerite de Valois, a rich and important lady. Vincent could be seen in the streets giving money to the poor, saying, "Here, a few pennies in the name of the queen!" In the hospital he would tell the sick: "Take this fruit from the queen!"

Vincent didn't know it yet, but a few years later he would be doing the same things out of love for Jesus.

Soon, however, false rumors were going around.
"You know, that Father Vincent de Paul who seems so generous is really a thief!"
"Impossible!"
"It's true. He stole money from a friend who lives with him!"
"I can't believe it!"
Vincent couldn't prove his innocence. He was ashamed of being accused so unfairly. This caused him to suffer for many years. Luckily, the real thief was arrested in the end.

Vincent was getting tired of chasing after riches and important people. He thought, "Why am I rushing around? Why does everything seem so empty and gloomy and lifeless? What do you want me to do, Lord?"

Vincent agreed to become the parish priest of Clichy, a poor parish. For the first time, twelve years after his ordination, he really served as a priest, instead of looking for honors. For the first time, he was happy!

One year later, the little parish of Clichy was all upset.
Their beloved pastor had just left. Everything had gone so well when he was there!
"We've never had a priest like him!"
"He repaired the church."
"Thanks to him I've learned to pray!"

Why did Father Vincent leave? Father de Berulle, his adviser, had found him a job as a private tutor in one of the most powerful families in the kingdom, the family of Count Philippe-Emmanuel de Gondi. At last Vincent felt he had found the special job he had so often dreamed of!
He shared the luxurious and dazzling life of the rich.

He taught catechism to the two older sons. He became a close friend of Mrs. de Gondi. He advised the count. Vincent felt that he was now very important.

Once Vincent was asked to visit a sick person in the country and hear his confession. Vincent was surprised at how little this man knew about religion. Before he died, the man said, "Now I can go home to God in peace!"

Mrs. de Gondi's heart was touched by this man. "Father Vincent," she said, "so many people need God! What can we do to teach them to know and love Jesus better, when they live so far out in the country?"

The two of them thought hard. Finally they came up with an idea. They would visit the farms, have priests preach in the churches, and invite the country people to ask God's forgiveness in the Sacrament of Penance. Vincent's first missionary sermon in one of the country parishes on January 25, 1617, was a great success. His simple, loving words touched everyone's heart. So many came to ask God's forgiveness that Vincent had to call other priests in to help hear confessions.

Things got moving. Vincent went from village to village preaching, listening, advising, and hearing confessions. This gave him the idea of gathering together and training priests who would dedicate their lives to these poor country people. This was the beginning of the Priests of the Mission, who are also called Vincentians.

Something had changed in Vincent's heart. He was happier talking about God to servants and farm workers than he was living in an atmosphere of wealth and comfort. He prayed hard. Little by little he began to understand that he must spend more time with poor people.

"What? I don't understand you, Father Vincent. You want to give up your important job with the Count's family?"

"Father de Berulle, in the country people are dying of hunger, and they are suffering because they don't know God. I can't live in this luxury any longer. I have decided to settle in a country parish where I can be close to the poor and take care of them."

And so, in July, 1617, Vincent became a country priest in the small town of Chatillon-les-Dombes!

One Sunday when he was getting ready for Mass, a lady came to see him. "Father," she reported, "a whole family is sick over in the neighborhood of Les Maladieres, out in the country. There is nobody to take care of them."

Vincent spoke with deep concern about this family to all the people who came to church. His parishioners set off to help the sick family, their arms full of packages and baskets of food.

That same evening Vincent gathered together a few dedicated women.

"Ladies," he told them, "all the gifts you collected for that poor family are very generous, but what will be left tomorrow? We must start organizing ourselves right now to do something more for the poor and the sick."

"How about all of us taking turns to go and see them?"

"What a good idea! The person whose turn it is will prepare dinner and take it to the sick. She will greet them, spread a napkin, and serve them, even feeding them if they can't feed themselves."

"But Father Vincent, that's how the rich are served, not the poor!"

"Exactly! You will serve for the love of Jesus. The poor will be your masters, and you will be their servants."

The enthusiastic conversation went on till late that night.
"Yes! We will do this work well — with all our hearts!"
"Whenever possible, try to bring meat to the sick people," added Vincent. "And while you are there, always try to cheer them up."
"Father Vincent, we could spend more time with those who are lonely."
"Yes, and above all remind them of how much Our Lord loves them. Lead them kindly to God. Now go, and do everything with love!"
This was the beginning of the Ladies of Charity.

Now Vincent's heart was filled with a burning fire:
"The love of Christ, the love of the poor."

He began to really live these words of Jesus,
"Whatever you do to others you do to me!"

After five months, the de Gondi family insisted that Vincent come back to work for them. He went on one condition: that they let him look after the poor and work against poverty. Count de Gondi was the general of the king's galleys and took Vincent with him to visit the prisoners. The king appointed Vincent to be the chaplain of the galleys in 1619.

Vincent was deeply upset by the situation of the convicts and galley slaves. These miserable prisoners received nothing but insults and punishments. They lived in very dirty conditions and were hungry and sick. They were the poorest of all! Vincent came with his Priests of the Mission to spend time with them.

Vincent spoke to Count de Gondi about the prisoners.
"Sir, we cannot leave these unfortunate people here in this galley!"
"They are convicts, Father Vincent!"
"But they are chained, and treated worse than animals. They should be given enough food and clothes. There should also be a clinic."
"And what else?"
Finally Vincent won. A light began to shine in the prisoners' misery.

Mrs. de Gondi became a Lady of Charity. As far away as Paris, many noble ladies were impressed by Father Vincent's enthusiasm for serving the poor.

In Paris in 1625, Vincent de Paul met Louise de Marillac, a noble, generous and religious lady. Together, she and Vincent would work marvels. Louise visited poor people in all kinds of weather and all sorts of places. She also encouraged and helped the Ladies of Charity when they had problems.

But not everything went smoothly.
"Father Vincent, these noble ladies of Paris are not used to work. They don't make soup and take it themselves into the slums. They send their servants. Servants do it because they're told to, not out of love!"
"How are things going for the poor people?"
"They're being treated roughly."
"That's a shame. We must find a solution!"

God himself found the solution!
One day Marguerite Naseau, a country girl, came to find Vincent. She told him how she wanted to help him serve his weakest brothers and sisters. Vincent sent her to Louise de Marillac. Other young girls soon joined her. Louise organized them and taught them to become real servants of the poor.

Vincent often encouraged them, saying, "My daughters, God looks down on you with joy. He is very pleased to see you carrying those baskets and pots of soup as if they were for him. The poor are your masters. Be sure to give them all they need. Most of all, tell them how precious they are to the heart of God." That was how the first Daughters of Charity were brought together and trained. The Sisters of Charity have also grown from this same tree.

Vincent's heart was touched especially by the suffering of little children. In 1628 in Paris, between 300 and 400 abandoned babies and children were found on street corners or near the churches. Some were taken to an orphanage. They were neglected and sometimes even sold to bad people. Many suffered a lot and died young.

Vincent talked to Louise de Marillac about their suffering:
"These children are dying in poverty. We have to help them!"
"Father Vincent, you could talk to the Ladies of Charity about them. They're meeting tomorrow."

The noble ladies began taking care of twelve children with the help of the Daughters of Charity. Five years later they had 1200 to bring up! They had to find ways to feed and clothe and teach them.

"What is the matter, ladies? You look worried!"
"Father Vincent, we can no longer pay enough baby-sitters, and we have no more bread."
"Don't be afraid. You took in these abandoned children as if they were your own. You have become their mothers. Be brave! The Lord will help you!"

And the sisters' work of caring for little children still continues today.

When Vincent's friend Francis de Sales asked him to help Jane de Chantal and her sisters, he also guided the Sisters of the Visitation.

Vincent was very often in Paris but also traveled around the countryside. He realized that the priests were not trained well enough to help the country people to know God. He said to himself, "These priests are all on their own. They need advice and help. I'm going to speak to some bishops about this."

Together they organized training sessions and seminaries where Vincent often went to speak to the priests and pray with them.

All these good works caused very important people to notice Vincent. When King Louis XIII died in 1643, Queen Anne called Vincent to the royal court to ask his advice. There was Vincent, from out in the country, sitting among the most important people in the kingdom: the queen, Prince de Conde, Cardinal Mazarin, and some bishops.

Vincent was wearing his old patched cassock, the same one he wore when he went to see the poor. Sometimes he was laughed at, especially by Cardinal Mazarin, who was jealous of his influence. "Ha! Ha!" he said, "Look at the beautiful clothes Father Vincent wears when he comes to court!" Vincent humbly laughed with the people who were laughing at him.

France was involved in a civil war. In the countryside bandits wrecked, killed and burned everything in their way. People had to escape from their villages. Vincent and his priests faced terrible dangers in coming to help them. On the battlefields and in the hospitals, the Daughters of Charity took care of the sick and the dying. More and more refugees were coming to Paris. Starvation and epidemics were everywhere. Vincent was very sad to see so much suffering.

One day, in the queen's presence, Vincent bravely asked Cardinal Mazarin for an important change.
"Your Eminence, give peace back to France! Leave your position of power and let the king return to Paris!"
"How dare you talk to me like that!" the cardinal cried. "That's enough! Go back to your poor!"
Vincent had to hide to escape the anger of the powerful Mazarin. But nothing would stop him from doing Jesus' work.

With all his followers, Vincent found a thousand ways to work against poverty. There was room in Vincent's huge heart for everyone... the sick, the poor, the elderly, the wounded, the handicapped, prisoners, orphans, the mentally ill, beggars, the unemployed. He wanted to give hope and joy back to everyone. He wanted to tell everyone about the great love of God.

Vincent's days were very full. To help the poor, train the Ladies and the Daughters of Charity and the Priests of the Mission, and advise all those who depended on him, he wrote thousands of letters, organized meetings, and looked after everyone constantly. Where did he find the strength to do this?

He found it in prayer: a prayer which started his day very early in the morning and accompanied him through to the evening.

Deep in his heart Vincent lived with God.

When he saw or heard something beautiful, he blessed God.

If he had an important decision to make, he made it with God.

When he was confused, he asked God to give him light and took the time to look for it in the Gospel. In Jesus he found the courage to carry on, and he gave all his strength right to the end.

Vincent wanted to make this love known to the ends of the earth! He sent Priests of the Mission to other countries, telling them, "Remember that you are called by God to carry his love everywhere, this divine fire!" ...as far as Italy, Poland, Madagascar, Ireland, even to the islands north of Scotland!

However Vincent's health was not as good as it seemed. He often had pain in his legs, and sometimes his whole body shook.

On September 27, 1660, when he was nearly eighty years old, he felt tired. During the night his friends sat him on his chair by the fire. He kissed the cross and pronounced for the last time the name of his Lord, whom he had served so faithfully in the poor: "Trust...Jesus..."

Vincent was proclaimed a saint in 1737.

Today Vincent is still with us through his spiritual sons and daughters and their work. His flame of love and service is still shining brightly, even as far away as China!

Today, all over the world, there are nearly two million persons who serve the poor as Vincent de Paul did: "In serving the poor, we serve Jesus Christ. Do everything with love."

Some interesting facts about Saint Vincent...

The words of Jesus which inspired the whole life of Saint Vincent de Paul are:

> "I was naked... I was hungry...
> I was lonely, sick or in prison...
> You gave me clothes and food...
> You came to see me and comfort me...
> What you have done
> to the most insignificant
> of my brothers and sisters,
> you have done to me.
> Come, good and faithful servant,
> enter into the joy of your Master."

(From chapter 25

of the Gospel of St. Matthew)

In Vincent's time sisters had to stay inside convents. Vincent dared to send the Daughters of Charity everywhere and so invented a new kind of religious life. He sent the sisters into slums which were sometimes dangerous, into hospitals, prisons and even onto battlefields, saying, "Your convent will be the houses of the sick, your cloister the streets of the town, your chapel the parish church." The Daughters of Charity were the first religious sisters to go out to teach country people, and the first visiting nurses, social workers, prison visitors, and teachers of children with special problems.

After Saint Vincent de Paul, God led many holy men and women to live in his spirit. Among the Priests of the Mission (Vincentians), the Daughters of Charity, and lay men and women you will find:

> Saint Catherine Labouré,
>
> Saint Jean-Gabriel Perboyre
> and Blessed Francois-Regis Clet,
> who were martyrs in China,
>
> Sister Rosalie Rendu,
>
> Blessed Frederic Ozanam,
> the father of a family,
>
> Saint Elizabeth Ann Seton,
> a wife, mother, widow,
> and foundress of the Sisters
> of Charity in the United States.

Each of them lived a life of prayer and special service to the poor.

A few words to help you better understand St. Vincent de Paul's life...

Cassock
Long garment worn by priests in Vincent's time.

Chaplain
Priest working especially in a place of worship other than a parish church, like a private chapel, prison, or hospital.

Count
Title for a noble person of wealth and importance in the kingdom.

Daughters of Charity
In Saint Vincent's time these were young girls from simple backgrounds (country or village people) who gave their whole life to God. They served the poor just like Saint Vincent, that is out of love for Jesus. Some are called Sisters of Charity.

Galley
Boat for war or freight, rowed by convicted prisoners, called "galley slaves."

Ladies of Charity
In Saint Vincent's time these were ladies from the nobility or the upper classes who served the poor as he did. They were married and mothers of families.

Master
Man who is served by another person or persons.

Porridge
Soft food, such as oatmeal, made of a grain and milk.

Priests of the Mission, Missionaries, Lazarists, Vincentians
These were the priests who were trained by Saint Vincent and sent everywhere by him to proclaim the love of God to everyone, but most especially to the poor. They are also called Lazarists because they lived at Saint Lazare in Paris. In the United States they are called Vincentian Fathers and Brothers.

Refugees
People who leave their homes to look for help, safety, or shelter in another place.

Seminary
Place of study and training for those who will become priests.

Your Eminence
Title used when talking to a Cardinal.

Prayer

*You do something wonderful, Lord,
when you place a spark of your love
deep in our hearts.*

*With your help,
a little shepherd boy became Father Vincent,
the man who promised to serve you
in every person he met.*

*Saint Vincent saw your face, Lord,
in the suffering, hunger, and tears
of so many poor and sick people.
He treated each one of them
just as he would have treated you.*

*Speak to me, Lord, I want to listen.
Fill my heart with your love.
Let me always use my hands, my feet,
and my voice to love and serve others.
Help me to spread peace and happiness
wherever I go.*

Amen.

BOOKS & MEDIA

The Daughters of St. Paul operate book and media centers at the following addresses. Visit, call or write the one nearest you today, or find us on the World Wide Web, www.pauline.org

CALIFORNIA
  3908 Sepulveda Blvd., Culver City, CA 90230; 310-397-8676
  5945 Balboa Ave., San Diego, CA 92111; 619-565-9181
  46 Geary Street, San Francisco, CA 94108; 415-781-5180
FLORIDA
  145 S.W. 107th Ave., Miami, FL 33174; 305-559-6715
HAWAII
  1143 Bishop Street, Honolulu, HI 96813; 808-521-2731
ILLINOIS
  172 North Michigan Ave., Chicago, IL 60601; 312-346-4228
LOUISIANA
  4403 Veterans Memorial Blvd., Metairie, LA 70006; 504-887-7631
MASSACHUSETTS
  50 St. Paul's Ave., Jamaica Plain, Boston, MA 02130; 617-522-8911
  Rte. 1, 885 Providence Hwy., Dedham, MA 02026; 781-326-5385
MISSOURI
  9804 Watson Rd., St. Louis, MO 63126; 314-965-3512
NEW JERSEY
  561 U.S. Route 1, Wick Plaza, Edison, NJ 08817; 732-572-1200
NEW YORK
  150 East 52nd Street, New York, NY 10022; 212-754-1110
  78 Fort Place, Staten Island, NY 10301; 718-447-5071
OHIO
  2105 Ontario Street, Cleveland, OH 44115; 440-621-9427
PENNSYLVANIA
  9171-A Roosevelt Blvd., Philadelphia, PA 19114; 215-676-9494
SOUTH CAROLINA
  243 King Street, Charleston, SC 29401; 843-577-0175
TENNESSEE
  4811 Poplar Ave., Memphis, TN 38117; 901-761-2987
TEXAS
  114 Main Plaza, San Antonio, TX 78205; 210-224-8101
VIRGINIA
  1025 King Street, Alexandria, VA 22314; 703-549-3806
CANADA
  3022 Dufferin Street, Toronto, Ontario, Canada M6B 3T5; 416-781-9131
  1155 Yonge Street, Toronto, Ontario, Canada M4T 1W2; 416-934-3440